PANZERS IN RUSSIA 1941-43

A PzKpfw III advances through a burning village
in north Russia, autumn 1941 (212/248/10A).

BRUCE QUARRIE
PANZERS IN RUSSIA 1941-43

WORLD
WAR
2
PHOTO
ALBUM
NUMBER 9

A selection of German wartime photographs
from the Bundesarchiv, Koblenz

 Patrick Stephens, Cambridge

First published in 1979

British Library Cataloguing in Publication Data

Panzers in Russia. 1941-43. – (World War 2
    photo albums; 9).
    1. World War, 1939-1945 – Campaigns –
    Russia – Pictorial works   2. Tanks
    (Military science) – History – Pictorial
    works
    1. Quarrie, Bruce   II. Series
    940.54'21   D757.54

    ISBN 0 85059 353 0
    ISBN 0 85059 354 9

Photoset in 10 pt Plantin Roman. Printed in Great
Britain on 100 gsm Pedigree coated cartridge and
bound by The Garden City Press Limited,
Letchworth, Hertfordshire SG6 1JS, for the
publishers, Patrick Stephens Limited, Bar Hill,
Cambridge, GB3 8EL

CONTENTS

Acknowledgement
The author and publisher would like to express their sincere thanks to Mrs Marianne Loenartz of the Bundesarchiv for her assistance, without which this book would have been impossible.

6

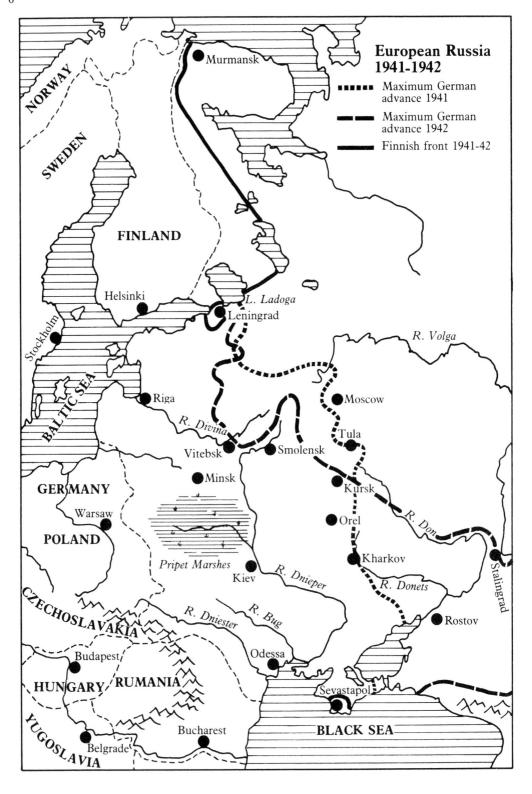

**European Russia
1941-1942**

▪▪▪▪ Maximum German
advance 1941

▬ ▬ Maximum German
advance 1942

▬▬ Finnish front 1941-42

7

Who won the war against Germany? There are several answers to this question depending upon your standpoint. The British can justifiably say that they did because, if they had not held out in 1940, nobody else would have had the opportunity. The Americans and Canadians can say that they did because, if it had not been for their aid, Britain could never have stood alone, and had it not been for their resources D-Day could never have taken place. But in the final analysis it is the Soviet Union which really has prior claim. It was Russian determination, fanaticism and, above all, sheer manpower, which defeated the Third Reich. Soviet propaganda texts naturally emphasise this fact, usually to the detriment of everyone else's efforts.

Although this is not really the place to go into the broad strategic considerations of World War 2, it is worth considering a few facts. And at the forefront of these must be the consideration that, had Hitler not decided upon his ill-advised onslaught on Russia, the whole of Europe would now probably be ruled from Berlin. This sounds a sweeping statement so let us examine it a little more closely.

At the close of 1940, German troops had occupied Poland, Norway, France and the Low Countries in a sequence of Blitzkrieg operations which literally astounded the world. Warfare quite like this had never been encountered before, although the principles were not new. Theoreticians among the European powers other than Germany had, as is the wont of most military minds in every age, planned for the last war rather than the next. The result was an over-reliance on fixed fortifications, field artillery and infantry with insufficient emphasis on the vital new weapons, the aircraft and the tank.

Only in Germany had the linked ideas of air power and highly mobile armoured forces gained serious consideration and, whatever else may be said about Hitler as a strategist, in this instance it cannot be denied that he was ahead of most of his contemporaries.

Thus it was that the static lines of defence fell, defeated by an enemy largely unconcerned about his flanks who was aiming at command and communications networks rather than wasting energy in simply killing the *Poilus* and Tommies in the front line.

However, having conquered virtually all of Western Europe, Hitler then made several disastrous mistakes. In the air war over Britain (see volumes 2 and 10 in this series) he and Göring allowed themselves to be distracted from the vital task of knocking out airfields and radar stations into pounding cities; while in the Mediterranean (see also volumes 1 and 7) he neglected to take out Malta directly after the fall of Greece and Crete, as he could so easily have done; and failed to keep the German forces in North Africa adequately supplied. It is always easy to be critical with the advantage of hindsight, but a concerted effort in this area by joint German/Italian forces could so easily have thrown the British out of the Mediterranean, and opened the path for a 'below the belt' punch at Russia through the Black Sea, that it is a miracle it never happened. Had Hitler concentrated on purely military rather than political considerations in this strategic context, it is my opinion that British *rapprochement* with or submission to Germany would have been an almost inevitable consequence in due course, despite naval superiority.

Without having to worry about his rear or his flanks, Hitler could have gone on to attack the Soviet Union with an excellent chance of success. As it was, he decided upon an attack when German aerial and naval forces were seriously pinned down in trying to keep Britain contained, while substantial numbers of troops, tanks, ships and aircraft, together with the services of one of his best generals, were tied down in North Africa.

Nevertheless, the initial stages of Operation Barbarossa, unleashed on June 22 1941, went even better than the German high command (OKW) had anticipated. Caught flat-footed, despite adequate warning from their intelligence sources, Soviet forces were sent reeling backwards during the opening days of the campaign, while huge numbers of their aircraft were destroyed in a lightning aerial strike only rivalled by that of the Israelis a quarter century later in 1967.

When I began researching the subject of 'Panzers in Russia' at the Bundesarchiv, it was with the full intention of putting the subject within the confines of a single volume, as with all the other books in this series. A couple of days' work soon showed the impracticality of this approach if the subject was to be done justice. For this reason it has been split into two books. This volume covers the campaign in Russia from the summer of 1941 until the early summer of 1943, prior to the Battle of Kursk, which was a major turning point in the war. Volume 12 in this series covers the later phases of the war in Russia. Thus this book predominantly illustrates early vehicles such as the PzKpfw II, PzKpfw III, PzKpfw 35(t) and 38(t), while the second volume contains mostly Tigers, Panthers, King Tigers and other members of the 'heavy brigade'.

The German armoured divisions amassed for the invasion of Russia were as follows:

Army Group North (von Leeb)
IV Panzer Group (Hoepner): 1st, 6th, and 8th Panzer Divisions.
Army Group Centre (von Bock)
II Panzer Group (Guderian): 3rd, 4th, 10th, 17th and 18th Panzer Divisions. III Panzer Group (Hoth): 7th, 12th, 19th and 20th Panzer Divisions.
Army Group South (von Rundstedt)
I Panzer Group (Kleist): 9th, 11th, 13th, 14th and 16th Panzer Divisions.
OKH Reserve (Stumme)
2nd and 5th Panzer Divisions.

Other formations which included integral AFV units were:

Army Group North – 3rd and 36th Motorised Infantry (Panzer-Grenadier) Divisions and SS Division 'Totenkopf' (Eicke); Army Group Centre – 1st Kavallerie Division, 10th, 14th, 18th, 20th and 29th Panzer-Grenadier Divisions, the élite 'Grossdeutschland' Division and the SS Division 'Reich' (Hausser); Army Group South – 16th and 25th Panzer-Grenadier Divisions plus SS Divisions Leibstandarte 'Adolf Hitler' (Dietrich) and 'Wiking' (Steiner); OKH Reserve – 60th Panzer-Grenadier Division.

At this stage of the war the 'standard' Panzer Division consisted of a tank brigade; a motorised infantry brigade; armoured reconnaissance, anti-tank, anti-aircraft, engineer and signals battalions and an artillery regiment, plus headquarters, medical and supply units, etc.

Each Panzer brigade theoretically comprised two regiments, each of two battalions.

The battalions were composed of three companies, two 'light' and one 'medium'. The mainstay of the light companies was the PzKpfw III, that of the medium companies the PzKpfw IV. Technical details of these vehicles can be found in the Appendix so I shall not weary the reader with repetition. A full-strength company was supposed to field 30 tanks, but the average number even at the beginning of the campaign was, in fact, closer to 20.

The 1st Panzer Division (Kirchner) had been formed in October 1935 in Weimar and had taken part in the invasions of Poland and France. The 2nd (Veiel) had been formed at the same time but in Würzburg and, in addition to the Polish and French Campaigns, had also been active in the Balkans in the spring of 1941. The 3rd Panzer Division (Model), also formed in October 1935, had seen similar action to the 1st. The 4th (von Langerman), created in Würzburg again but three years later, had also fought in Poland and France prior to the invasion of Russia.

The 5th Panzer Division (Fehn), created in November 1938 in Oppeln, had fought in France, Yugoslavia and Greece. The 6th (Landgraf), formed from the 1st Light Division in October 1939, had fought in France and was to spearhead Army Group North's assault in June 1941. The famous 7th Panzer Division (von Funck), formed at the same time from the 2nd Light Division, had previously been commanded by Rommel in France. The 8th (Brandenberger) had also been established in October 1939 (from the 3rd Light Division) and, after fighting in France, had been transferred to Yugoslavia where, however, it played an inactive role.

The 9th Panzer Division (Hubicki) was not formed until January 1940, from the 4th Light Division, but was active in Belgium (including Dunkerque) in 1940 and later in the Balkans. The 10th (Schaal) had been created earlier, in April 1939 in Prague, and had fought in Poland and France. The 11th (Crüwell) had been formed from the 11th Rifle Brigade in August 1940 and had only seen battle in the Balkans prior to Russia. The 12th (Harpe) had been formed even later, in October 1940, from the 2nd Motorised Infantry Division, and saw its first combat in Russia.

The 13th Panzer Division (von Rothkirch) had been formed in Rumania from the 13th Motorised Infantry Division in October 1940 as a training unit, and also drew blood for the first time in Russia. The 14th (Kühn), formed in August 1940 from the 4th Infantry Division, had seen prior combat in Yugoslavia, while the 16th (Hube), created at the same time, had been held in reserve during the Balkan campaign. The 17th (von Arnim), 18th (Nehring), 19th (von Knobelsdorff) and 20th (Stumpf) Panzer Divisions were all established in October 1940 and saw their first action in Russia. Thus, with seven exceptions, all the German Panzer Divisions were manned by blooded veterans with a record of sweeping success, and optimism was high that Russia would also be a walkover . . . although there were those who looked at the immense distances shown on their maps and wondered.

The three Army Groups had been assigned initial tasks as follows: in the north, von Leeb was to take the Baltic ports, including Leningrad; in the centre the immediate objective was Smolensk; while in the south von Rundstedt had Kiev and the Dnieper crossings as his first challenge.

In the north Hoepner's Group, divided into two Panzer Korps under Manstein and Reinhardt, made rapid progress through the former independent state of Lithuania (where they were welcomed as liberators from the Stalinist yoke) and were across the River Dvina by June 27. Here they had only been faced by seven Russian divisions, since the bulk of Soviet resistance was in the south.

There, von Rundstedt – lacking the armoured resources of the centre and north – could only make relatively slow headway. Kiev was not entered (by 13th Panzer Division) until mid-July, and the Russians still held the Dnieper bridges in strength. This situation produced a fatal error on Hitler's behalf. He transferred vital troops from the centre to help out.

In the centre, Guderian's three Panzer Korps commanded by von Gerr, von Vietinghoff and Lemelsen, had reached Minsk by the same date Hoepner's tanks were rolling across the Dvina. By the time Kleist was in Kiev, they were in Smolensk. Responding to the situation in the south, therefore, rather than allowing Army Group Centre to concentrate on its second objective, Moscow, Hitler diverted thousands of men and vehicles from Guderian's command to link up with Kleist's in a vast encircling operation around Kiev. This resulted in a sweeping German victory with huge numbers of Soviet troops taken prisoner. But, coupled with the diversion of Panzer Group III to the north to aid Hoepner, this manoeuvre slowed the German centre's impetus and gave the Russians time to prepare elaborate defences in front of Moscow.

Like their western allies, the Russians had relied overmuch on static fortifications to slow an aggressor but, with such a long border, this type of linear defence could not hope to succeed. It would have required far better organised mobile reserves than the Russians possessed to stop the fast-moving Panzers. Nevertheless, the very heavily armoured KV–I and –II tanks created havoc whenever they appeared, since their 75–120 mm main armour was totally impervious to the standard German 3·7 cm and 5 cm anti-tank guns. These monsters had thus to be immobilised (for example, by stripping a track) in order that they could then be eliminated at point-blank range. The only German weapon which was really effective against Russian heavy tanks (until the advent of the 7·5 cm Pak 40) was the Flak 88, and this was always in short supply.

The Germans first encountered genuine Russian armoured resistance on June 26 when the KV tanks tried to intercept Reinhardt's Korps near Rossienie. They were, however, defeated due to superior German communications (very few Russian tanks were radio-equipped) and manoeuvreability allowing the 1st, 6th and 8th Panzer Divisions to cross the Dvina. Pushing on towards Ostrov, Army Group North penetrated the so-called Stalin Line but, after capturing the town on July 4 had to face a stiff counter-attack which was only halted by massed artillery fire. After capturing Pskov three days later the Panzer divisions had opened the road to Leningrad. However, Russian resistance was stiffening, the roads were becoming increasingly bad, and forests, marshes and minefields further slowed the advance.

A fierce three-day battle developed in the vicinity of Solzy/Novgorod in which the Soviet 11th Army was defeated, but Hoepner's mechanised forces were by this time in bad need of extensive maintenance and OKW ordered a three-week pause. Unfortunately, this also gave the Russians time to catch their breath and prepare further defences, but to begin with German obstinacy prevailed and Hoepner's tanks were out of the most densely wooded part of north-western Russia and well on the road to

Leningrad by mid-August. Despite renewed Russian counter-attacks, which took severe toll of the Panzer divisions, by early September they were through the city's outer defensive ring and on the 11th the 1st Panzer Division took the Duderhofer Hills, from which the Germans could peer into the heart of the city itself. Here, however, the advance ended for all practical purposes. The reinforcements which had been assigned to Army Group North were stripped for Operation 'Taifun' – the belated assault on Moscow – and the capture of Leningrad itself was accorded a lower priority. Thus began one of the epic sieges of all time.

Guderian's group in the centre, after having captured hundreds of thousands of Russian troops in the early encirclements around Bialystock, Minsk and Smolensk, had been diverted to help out in the south. Bad weather and intermittent but strong Soviet resistance hindered his advance, but by the time Army Group North was fighting its way into the outskirts of Leningrad, von Kleist had begun closing the southern arm of the pincer movement around Kiev. Kleist and Guderian joined hands on September 14, closing the pocket, the net result being the capture of some 650,000 Russian troops and enormous stocks of war material. But by the time Hitler agreed to renew the offensive against Moscow on the 21st, too much time had been lost.

At the beginning of Operation Taifun, the Soviet forces concentrated around Moscow were taken by surprise, and in two further encircling operations around Briansk and Viasma the Russian commander, Yeremenko, lost over 700,000 troops, 1,000 AFVs and 5,000 guns. These disasters could have opened the gates of Moscow to the fast-moving Panzers, but then the Russian weather came to the rescue of Communism: heavy and prolonged rain turned the unsurfaced Russian roads into quagmires of mud which made any form of movement a veritable nightmare, and the Germans lost the advantage of their mobility. At the same time, a new Soviet commander was appointed to head the defence of the capital – Zhukov.

In mid-November frost turned the muddy roads to iron and the Germans were again able to move, but the bright weather did not last long and heavy snow, coupled with freezing fog and increased Soviet resistance, finally brought them to a reluctant halt a mere 40-odd miles from their goal. Other factors, of course, played a part; vehicle unserviceability for one. Even the lightest grade oils were sluggish in the temperatures now being experienced and the anti-freeze was having little effect. The Russians, used to their own climate, normally try to play down the effect of this severe weather on German plans and attribute the salvation of Moscow purely to the heroism of its defenders. Without decrying the latter, it is impossible in an apolitical history to ignore the former.

However, while Army Group North had come to a grinding halt outside Leningrad and their companions in the centre had reached a similar impasse in front of Moscow, the initially slow advance in the south had made great strides. After the joint operation around Kiev with Guderian's troops, resistance in the southern theatre of operations seemed almost to melt away – with the exception of the fortified Soviet positions in the Crimea. Reinforced by allied units – Italians and Hungarians – the Germans continued their advance across the Ukrainian steppes and, by the middle of November, were approaching Rostov on Don. But the names of Stalino and Dnepropetrovsk will live on in the memories of those troops involved in this theatre as the Russians launched a heavy counter-attack during the winter which forced the Germans back to the line of the River Msus.

The winter of 1941–42 was, in fact, critical on all fronts and German publications tend to skirt round it. Vast tracts of ground were recaptured by the Russians, particularly in the north where they succeeded in driving a wedge between Army Groups North and Centre which opened out into a huge salient – not unlike the later Kursk situation. Around Leningrad the besiegers were themselves besieged, while in front of Moscow the invaders were pushed back to a line running roughly from Orel to Smolensk, with a narrow finger of occupied territory thrusting northwards precariously into the recaptured ground. Tough Siberian troops, acclimatised and well equipped for the rigours of winter war, together with increasing numbers of the famous T–34 tank, were principally responsible.

Although there are exponents for the Panther, the Tiger and other tanks, the concensus is that the T–34 was the best tank produced during World War 2, and its continued front-line existence in many Soviet-aligned countries to this date is certain testimony to the soundness of its basic design. The features which spring most readily to mind are its well-sloped armour plate, designed to deflect solid armour-piercing shells; and its wide tracks which gave it an exceptional cross-country performance, particularly in muddy or wintry conditions.

Armed initially with a 76·2 mm L/30·5 gun (for which 80 rounds of ammunition were carried) and later by longer-barrelled versions as well as by the 85 mm M–1944 L/51·5, the T–34 had all-round armour 40 to 45 mm thick and could cover 130 miles cross-country at an average speed of 25 mph – a very good factor for the time. Carrying a crew of four, it weighed 26 tons. The chief criticisms of it are the paucity of communications equipment, lack of crew comfort (which enhances battle fatigue) and the large turret hatch which was, however, replaced on later versions by a cupola.

Certainly German designers were impressed by the T–34, and the later Panther and King Tiger owe much to it in their parentage. Yet where can you see either being used on today's battlefields?

Aided by improved Soviet armoured tactics, the T–34 was really to come into its own during 1942 when the Russians were able to hold the northern and central fronts in virtual stalemate. Only in the south were German forces able to make any real headway.

After repelling a Russian attack in May, the reorganised Army Groups A and B under List and von Bock which now constituted the southern force rapidly captured Voronezh. The recalcitrant city of Sevastopol also fell at the beginning of July after another epic siege, and the German Panzers pressed on rapidly towards their new goal – the rich oilfields surrounding the Caucasus mountains. With some justification, Hitler had reasoned that, if he could not bring the Stalinist bear to its knees by crippling its communications centres, he could do so equally well by crippling its POL* supplies. But once again political 'necessity' had intruded upon military necessity. During the preceding winter Hitler had dismissed, replaced or relegated several of his best Panzer commanders – including Guderian, of all people! – and replaced them with less argumentative sycophants, thus paving the way for the disaster of Stalingrad.

* Petrol, Oil and Lubricants.

Stalingrad in itself was not a particularly strategically important objective, yet because of the name the town bore both sides were determined to make it a memorial to their determination and courage. The thousands who needlessly lost their lives within its barren confines must still curse its name.

On this southern front, the German soldier encountered a totally new world, comparable to that discovered by Alexander the Great's troops so many centuries before when they, too, were thrusting into the unknown Orient. Heat, dust, flies; strange beasts with deformed backs and vicious tempers; wild, semi-nomadic tribesmen straight out of mediaeval legend; and endless, flat steppe until, like a mirage floating on the horizon, the distant peaks of the cool and lonely Caucasus mountains flickered in the haze.

Picture yourself in a German tank at this point in time. The tracks rattle constantly beneath you, adding their clangorous squeak to the coughing roar of the Maybach engine. Clouds of dust envelope you as the dry grasses and sunbaked soil are churned into hay fever-provoking fog around you. The constant jolting and rattling, coupled with a heat level that Hitler's Germany had never known and the constant buzzing irritation of innumerable insects makes sleep or, indeed, any form of rest almost impossible. Then there is the smell of diesel or petrol fumes and, in battle, the pitch and roll of your tank as it tries to 'do' while avoiding being 'done by'; the metallic clangour of empty shell cases being ejected from the gun breech and rolling around the turret basket floor; the mercilessly ear-piercing stammer of the 7·92 mm MG 34 machine-gun, more painful than the barely heard 'crack' of the main gun firing its lethal hardware at a distant target. Dust, heat, noise, stink. 'Heil Hitler!' but pity the poor b. . . . y infantry who have had to walk the last 300 miles.

This is not an overworked author's imagination getting the better of him. I have done both, on 'live' exercise, in Canada, with 105 mm shells cracking overhead and fragments of shrapnel burying themselves into the ground six inches in front of my boot; with the sun burning down on an empty wasteland tenanted only by snakes and ground squirrels, and the nearest beer 50 miles away! The mud on a cold and misty morning on Salisbury Plain is even worse.

Inside the illusory shelter of a tank, heat and cold are often worse enemies than the enemy.

As the summer of 1942 advanced, the sheer distances being covered by the German forces began to create their own problems, namely supply and maintenance, while improving Soviet tactical sophistication made impossible the vast encirclements of the previous year. Nevertheless, Rostov was recaptured and 4th Panzer Army pressed on to the oilfield at Maikop – where they found that the Russians had destroyed all the drilling and refining equipment.

The slow-moving forces in Von Paulus' 6th Army, meanwhile, were inexorably marching towards their appointment with destiny at Stalingrad. Here the Russian defence attained truly heroic proportions. Every building was turned into a veritable strongpoint which had to be conquered individually. After two months of bitter fighting nine-tenths of the city was in German hands, but still the tenacious defenders refused to give up.

Marshal Zhukov saw in the German preoccupation with Stalingrad an excellent opportunity to effect an encirclement of his own and, while the house-to-house fighting continued in the city, began preparing a massive counter-attack. Vainly von Paulus appealed to Hitler to be allowed to pull back to a more defensible position.

Zhukov's hammer fell on November 17 and put the reluctant troops of the Rumanian armies north and south of Stalingrad into rout, allowing Soviet troops to completely encircle the city and von Paulus' army. The German troops were ill-equipped to withstand a siege since, for the most part, they lacked adequate winter clothing and the sub-zero temperatures added their debilitating effect to the strain of battle. Göring's boast that he could keep the troops supplied from the air was soon shown to be hollow, and the plight of the German forces became increasingly desperate.

A brave attempt by von Manstein to relieve the city in December failed because von Paulus felt constrained by Hitler's 'stand fast' orders. Nevertheless, von Paulus succeeded in holding out until January 31 1943 when, with half his men dead of wounds, cold, starvation and disease, he was finally forced to surrender.

Earlier in the same month the Russians had launched a new counter-offensive which fell on the hapless 2nd Hungarian Army and opened a 200-mile gap in the German lines east of Kharkov. Manstein was forced to withdraw from Rostov by this threat to his flank, while von Kleist was compelled to withdraw his Army Group A by sea from the Taman Peninsular to the Crimea.

Further north, the Russians succeeded in encircling two of 2nd Army's three Korps which were withdrawing in an orderly manner west of Voronezh. Manstein attempted to stem the tide at Kharkov but was forced to relinquish his grasp on that city also. Now, however, the Russians made a grave mistake. In their eagerness they poured the six tank Corps commanded by Popov into the gap created in the German line, but these forces were in turn cut off by Manstein and von Kleist, attacking simultaneously from north and south, while Hausser's SS Panzer Korps succeeded in recapturing Kharkov (see also No 3 in this series, *Waffen-SS in Russia*).

With the front thus stabilised the Germans were able to turn their attention to the last remaining Soviet salient around the small and hitherto unimportant town of Kursk, and both sides began amassing forces for what was to prove one of the most crucial battles in the war. Full details appear in volume 12 of this series.

The photographs in this book have been selected with care from the Bundesarchiv, Koblenz (the approximate German equivalent of the US National Archives or the British Public Records Office). Particular attention has been devoted to choosing photographs which will be fresh to the majority of readers, although it is inevitable that one or two may be familiar. Other than this, the author's prime concern has been to choose good-quality photographs which illustrate the type of detail that enthusiasts and modellers require. In certain instances quality has, to a degree, been sacrificed in order to include a particularly interesting photograph. For the most part, however, the quality speaks for itself.

The Bundesarchiv files hold some one million black and white negatives of Wehrmacht and Luftwaffe subjects, including 150,000 on the Kriegsmarine, some 20,000 glass negatives from the inter-war period and several hundred colour photographs. Sheer numbers is one of the problems which makes the compilation of a book such as this difficult. Other difficulties include the fact that, in the vast majority of cases, the negatives have not been printed so the researcher is forced to look through box after box of 35 mm contact strips – some 250 boxes containing an average of over 5,000 pictures each, plus folders containing a further 115,000 contact prints of the Waffen-SS; moreover, cataloguing and indexing the negatives is neither an easy nor a short task, with the result that, at the present time, Luftwaffe and Wehrmacht subjects as well as entirely separate theatres of operations are intermingled in the same files.

There is a simple explanation for this confusion. The Bundesarchiv photographs were taken by war correspondents attached to German military units, and the negatives were originally stored in the Reich Propaganda Ministry in Berlin. Towards the close of World War 2, all the photographs – then numbering some $3\frac{1}{2}$ million – were ordered to be destroyed. One man in the Ministry, a Herr Evers, realised that they should be preserved for posterity and, acting entirely unofficially and on his own initiative, commandeered the first available suitable transport – two refrigerated fish trucks – loaded the negatives into them, and set out for safety. Unfortunately, one of the trucks disappeared en route and, to this day, nobody knows what happened to it. The remainder were captured by the Americans and shipped to Washington, where they remained for 20 years before the majority were returned to the government of West Germany. A large number, however, still reside in Washington. Thus the Bundesarchiv files are incomplete, with infuriating gaps for any researcher. Specifically, they end in the autumn of 1944, after Arnhem, and thus record none of the drama of the closing months of the war.

The photographs are currently housed in a modern office block in Koblenz, overlooking the River Mosel. The priceless negatives are stored in the basement, and there are strict security checks on anyone seeking admission to the Bildarchiv (Photo Archive). Regrettably, and the author has been asked to stress this point, the archives are *only open to bona fide authors and publishers, and prints can only be supplied for reproduction in a book or magazine.* They CANNOT be supplied to private collectors or enthusiasts for personal use, so *please* – don't write to the Bundesarchiv or the publishers of this book asking for copy prints, because they cannot be provided. The well-equipped photo laboratory at the Bundesarchiv is only capable of handling some 80 to 100 prints per day because each is printed individually under strictly controlled conditions – another reason for the fine quality of the photographs but also a contributory factor in the above legislation.

THE PHOTOGRAPHS

Left Impressed French Hotchkiss tanks photographed near Luga on March 21 1942. Note the Panzer beret still being worn at this late date (78/109/3A).

Above PzKpfw IVs of Nehring's 18th Panzer Division roll across the Beresina during the drive on Smolensk, July 3 1941 (75/79/19).

Below A PzKpfw IIB of the 17th Panzer Division knocked out on July 14 1941 (75/78/22A).

Above Elements of the 29th Panzer Grenadier Division's reconnaissance unit near Baranovitch on July 2 1941 (78/109/6A).

Left An SdKfz 221 light armoured car of the same unit with Russian prisoners, also photographed on July 2 1941 (78/109/7A).

Above right PzKpfw III command vehicle of Kuhn's 14th Panzer Division which has proved too heavy for this wooden bridge in the Ukraine, September 14 1941 (75/78/25A). This photo has been incorrectly identified elsewhere as belonging to the 5th Panzer Division.

Right 8·8 cm Flak gun and detachment photographed in the Ukraine in July 1941. Note barrel clamp and breech cover still in place (78/109/5A).

Left Personnel of a Luftwaffe heavy Flak unit unload 8·8 cm shells from an SdKfz 7 half-track south-west of Stalino in the Ukraine in October 1941. I have been unable to identify the oakleaf and acorns device from my own references, although the oakleaf suggests 1st Panzer Division which was operating in the north! (78/109/9A).

Below Laying the sights of a leFH 18 outside Leningrad on November 3 1941 (78/109/1A).

Right SdKfz 251/1 fitted with Schwerer Wurfrahmen 40 to fire six 28/32 cm rockets. The unit device identifies it as an 8th Panzer Division vehicle on the northern front (208/21/39A).

Below right SdKfz 11 half-track towing a 10·5 cm leFH 18 field howitzer (208/19/11).

Left PzKpfw 35(t)s on the northern front (208/31/3).

Below left PzKpfw 35(t) in a Russian forest (208/29/25).

Right Panzer pioneer in Russia wearing the unique black and white waffenfarbe which was rarely seen after 1940 (208/21/25A).

Below Interesting shot of a 'motormart' near Roslavl in September 1941. The 'piston man' device is that of Spare Parts Detachment (Ersatzteilstaffel) 205 (78/109/2A).

Left Said to have been photo-graphed on the northern front, this picture shows an SdKfz 231 armoured car (205/1800/32).

Below SdKfz 251 half-tracks belonging to the 8th Panzer Division (208/22/16).

Right This dramatic night shot shows a 15 cm sFH 18 firing, possibly on the Leningrad front (206/1866/11).

Below right PzKpfw IV (left) with a knocked-out Russian KV-1 (208/29/4).

Inset above Good detail shot of the headphones on this much-decorated Panzer NCO which will be especially useful to modellers (209/74/6A).

Inset above right Driver's position in an SdKfz 251 (209/53/15).

Background photograph Searching for a way around a burning village, SdKfz 250 half-tracks and PzKpfw IIIs, believed to be of the 3rd Panzer Division, pause in the road (209/81/21).

Left German officers inspect a massive Soviet KV-2 which has come to grief in a swamp (209/71/10).

Below Infantry and a PzKpfw IVD pause in sight of a blazing Russian farm (209/90/26).

Right Other than the turret number '402' on the nearest vehicles, no markings can be discerned on these PzKpfw IVs of Army Group North (209/74/12A).

Far right Generalmajor Walter Krüger (left) confers with General der Panzer Truppen Reinhardt, commander of Panzer Korps XLI in the north (209/76/1A).

Below right Only 74 PzKpfw IBs participated in Operation Barbarossa. These were photographed in Lithuania (208/23/5).

Above The blazing remains of a T-28 multi-turretted medium/heavy tank (209/94/5).

Below Although fast, the BT-7 light/medium tanks were no match for the German PzKfw IIIs and IVs (209/56/27).

Above Rare picture of a captured Russian STV Komsomolets artillery tractor (209/61/20A).

Below 8·8 cm Flak with two 'kill' markings on its barrel deployed in the anti-tank role (209/71/7).

Left SdKfz 253 observation vehicle of the 1st Panzer Division in the north. It carries the tactical sign of a towed artillery unit (209/56/20).

Below 5 cm Pak 38 L/60 anti-tank gun (209/79/19).

Right PzKpfw 38(t)s investigate a farm (267/139/25A).

Below right A PzKpfw III and its prey (268/157/35).

Above left PzKpfw IIIs carrying the white 'G' of Guderian's group and the bison device of the 10th Panzer Division (213/261/2A).

Left PzKpfw IIIG with one of Guderian's divisions (212/243/27).

Above PzKpfw IIb towing a trailer containing a drum of fuel. Very few of these early Mark IIs took part in the invasion. This reconnaissance (Aufklärungs) vehicle is from the 12th Panzer Division which operated under Hoth in the centre (265/3/14A).

Right German signpost pointing north to Witebsk, west to Minsk and east to Moscow (267/104/33A).

Inset above left A battery of sFH 18 howitzers being emplaced and camouflaged (209/87/5).

Inset above Obsolete Russian Austin-Putilov armoured car knocked out in the early fighting (209/78/3).

Background photograph German infantry attack a Russian strongpoint under covering artillery fire (209/71/35).

These two pages and overleaf To protect the vital railways from partisan attacks, the Germans used many improvised armoured trains such as the example shown here. The infantry lay in lightly armoured flatbed trucks, accompanied by one or more tanks – usually of obsolete or captured design, such as this French Somua S-35. Once partisan activity was detected, the train would halt to allow the tank(s) to descend, with supporting infantry, to hunt them down. In these scenes a Wehrmacht cine cameraman seems to be having some difficulties! (212/209/5, 9, 10, 14, 16 and 32).

Left and below (See caption on page 36).

Right and below right The Czech PzKpfw 35 (t) was also widely used. Here an infantry section hitch a ride, prepared to duck down behind if they come under fire. Note Russian anti-tank obstacles spaced too far apart to be effective (210/143/6A and 210/146/23A).

Above PzKpfw IVD crossing a pontoon bridge (210/108/8).

Left The most potent adversary faced by German armour was the T-34. This early example armed with a 76·2 mm gun and photographed during the muddy autumn of 1941 has been captured and impressed into German service (213/296/5).

Above right Conglomeration of armour – PzKpfw IIs, IIIs and IVs in a Russian village (271/308/6).

Right One of the sights of Kharkov – a First World War British tank stands as a memorial (267/106/34).

Above left A very rare beast indeed, a PzKpfw II (Flamm), a conversion of the Ausf D which had a single MG 34 in the turret and two flame projectors above the front track guards (268/159/14).

Left The 'Y' of 7th Panzer Division dominates this array of signposts, past which a PzKpfw III of the 10th Panzer Division is trundling. Interestingly, this vehicle carries both the 'alternative' bison device on its turret and the divisional 'Y with three bars' on its hull front, together with the unusual single turret number '5' in outline form and the smaller numbers '621' in white upon what appears to be a black lozenge, making a colourful subject for modellers (214/336/2).

Above German mortar team in the blazing ruins of a Russian village (213/278/26).

Right An SdKfz 265, an armoured command vehicle based on the PzKpfw IB with extra radio equipment (265/6/16).

Background photograph The rigours of the Russian winter made mobile operations extremely difficult! (213/264/14).

Inset above Spare boots slung around his neck, this infantryman is at least sensibly dressed for the weather. The photo is said to have been taken at Pesotschnya on March 11 1942 (78/109/4A).

Inset above right Unloading supplies from pontoon barges beside a partially frozen river (thought to be the Volga) (268/172/25).

Left PzKpfw 38(t) of Panzer Regiment 21 displaying the 'early' 20th Panzer Division device on its rear hull (213/267/13).

Below A PzKpfw I of the 10th Panzer Division. The car in the background also displays the division's white-outlined bison device, the symbol of Panzer Regiment 7 (213/269/31A).

Right PzKpfw II of the 11th Panzer Division bogged down in the autumnal mud (213/271/19A).

Centre right PzKpfw IICs in Smolensk (213/257/5).

Below right French Renault R35 with the name 'Lotti' painted on its front assists a truck which has got stuck in a ditch (271/344/19).

Left Unfortunately, no identifying insignia can be seen on these PzKpfw IVs in Russia (268/185/3A).

Below Outside Leningrad, the Germans dug in for a prolonged siege (214/339/22).

Right A cold lunch for this motorcyclist, who is resting his feet on his BMW's cylinders for warmth (214/313/12).

Below right 15 cm sIG (Sf) auf PzKpfw IB serving with the 8th Panzer Division (215/398/21A).

Left The 3rd Panzer Division's bear device can clearly be seen on this truck's mudguard (217/470/26).

Below SdKfz 221 in the foreground, with a 223 radio car and a 222 heading the convoy (267/142/10).

Right Eventually the thaw came and the advance could continue. Here PzKpfw IVs ford a stream (268/157/9).

Below right PzKpfw IIIs cross a frozen river. In the background are some 20 mm Flakvierling anti-aircraft guns on half-track chassis (218/544/19).

Above left A German infantryman 'searches' the commander
of a Russian T-26 in this very
posed shot (267/115/26).

Left PzKpfw III displaying a
prominent aerial recognition
flag on its turret bin
(219/595/22).

Above Quad 20 mm Flakvierling being towed behind a truck,
summer 1942 (220/636/22).

Right Stug III armed with the
long-barrelled 7·5 cm gun, unit
a n d   d a t e   u n k n o w n
(220/602/19).

Background photograph Low-flying Ju 87 Stuka returns from a sortie above a trio of German tanks. The foreground vehicle is a PzKpfw II, behind which are two PzKpfw IVs with short-barrelled 7·5 cm guns, while on the right is a PzKpfw IV with the long-barrelled gun (216/403/34A).

Inset right PzKpfw IVs of the 11th Panzer Division ford a stream (211/198/20).

Inset below right PzKpfw IVF1 in the south. The crew are all wearing sun goggles, but no unit identifying devices are apparent (216/445/18).

Left PzKpfw IIIJ with 5 cm L/60 gun, probably in the south (215/398/36A).

Below left Motor cycle reconnaissance unit of the 1st Kavallerie Division (24th Panzer Division) (216/447/14).

Right Plucking the lunch! Men of Panzer Regiment 3, 2nd Panzer Division, with their prey. The regiment's winged serpent device, outlined white within a Panzer grey shield, is believed to have been either red or green (212/247/34).

Below SdKfz 251 liberally covered with foliage as camouflage on the steppe (216/413/25).

Left Light armoured cars of a reconnaissance unit within the 1st Kavallerie Division. In the foreground is an SdKfz 222 (216/424/10A).

Below left PzKpfw III J of the 9th Panzer Division (216/430/18A).

Above right Still smoking, the wreck of a KV-1 (216/412/10).

Right PzKfw III L on the steppe (216/416/18).

Below Miscellaneous PzKpfw IVs on the move across country. No unit markings are visible, but the foreground vehicle is an Ausf F2 (216/413/21).

Left PzKpfw IVF2 and StuG III of an unidentified unit (217/480/24).

Below left 7th Panzer Division PzKpfw II heading a convoy of trucks (265/8/27).

Right PzKpfw IIFs and a vast, empty horizon (212/491/13A).

Below End of a T-34 (217/485/20).

Inset above left MG 34 position on the outskirts of Sevastopol (231/721/12A).

Inset above General Hoth (centre) with Oberst iig von Natzmer (right) and an unidentified Oberleutnant on the bank of the River Don (217/451/16).

Background photograph Dramatic shot of a StuG III in a burning village, late 1942 (275/583/31A).

Above left PzKpfw IIIJs with the L/42 version of the 5 cm gun (218/504/26).

Left A heavily laden PzKpfw II escorting a convoy of supply vehicles across a causeway (217/469/26).

Above Although action does not seem to be imminent, this 7·5 cm Pak 40 gunner is keeping a good watch on the horizon (217/478/22).

Right A drink of milk for the crew of a patchily camouflaged SdKfz 251 (217/495/6A).

Above Good picture of an SdKfz 222 light armoured car (275/558/15).

Below 1st Kavallerie Division on the move. Visible are PzKpfw IIs, IIIs and IVs and an SdKfz 251 (218/510/22).

Above 20 mm Flak mounted on a Demag light half-track of the 1st Kavallerie Division (218/507/10).

Below Probably photographed in the late summer of 1942, this early Marder III is equipped with a captured and rebored Russian 76·2 mm gun (218/526/26).

Left General Scherer (left) in a trench with his troops. In the foreground is one of the improvised 'multiple' grenades used for trench assaults (274/493/22).

Below left A PzKpfw IIIJ of the 1st Kavallerie Division in Stalingrad, this one featuring 20 mm additional armour on its superstructure front (218/525/5).

Right General der Panzer Truppen Reinhardt and General-Major Trant (275/551/10A).

Below General FeldMarschall von Richtofen with Generals Kempf and Hoth (216/410/8).

Above and left PzKpfw IIIs and IVs of the 1st Kavallerie division on the Stalingrad front (218/524/6 and 220/601/9).

Above right and right 1st Kavallerie Division PzKpfw IIIJs outside Stalingrad (218/522/13 and 218/528/6).

Inset left Infantry and a PzKpfw III pause during the bitter fighting for the city (218/528/31).

Inset right A mortar team entrenching beside the protective bulk of a disabled T-34 in Stalingrad (218/529/17).

Background photograph Panoramic view of the magical city of Stalingrad (218/523/34).

Above Bactrian camels were one of the exotic sights as German troops entered southern Asiatic Russia! (217/455/24).

Left Infantry hitch a lift on a PzKpfw III, autumn 1942 (217/467/33A).

Above right Building a pontoon bridge over a narrow stretch of the Don (217/451/13).

Right This gun is so well camouflaged it is difficult to identify, especially as there is nothing to give it scale, but my guess is a 21 cm Mrs 18 (269/208/36).

Above left Tiger I entrained for the front. Note that it is fitted with its narrow transport tracks, the combat tracks being rolled on the front of the wagon (220/630A/24A).

Left A Panzer Oberleutnant confers with an infantry Hauptmann (269/221/7).

Above An attractive model diorama subject, perhaps, is this PzKpfw IV well and truly bogged down in a half-frozen stream (268/176/18).

Right German armoured train brought to grief when partisans succeeded in wrecking the bridge over which it was passing (217/460/2). The locomotive itself is Russian.

Opposite page and above
Motor cycle reconnaissance unit of the 24th Panzer Division comes under fire from a Russian farmhouse – the troops take cover then fan out to attack (216/447/15, 16 and 17).

Right The remains of a Russian village (213/260/29A).

Left and below Good shots of a PzKpfw IVG probably taken during the winter of 1942. Unfortunately no divisional markings are apparent which leaves the badge on the turret rather a mystery, unless some reader has better references than myself (273/446/26 and 29).

Right Infantry (pioneers?) on skis carry their tools on an improvised sledge past a line of PzKpfw IVs (215/351/33).

Below right Lease-Lend M3 Lee tank supplied to Russia by the United States and here captured by the Germans: it carries three sets of markings – 'USA 304850' on the hull rear, the Soviet number '147' on the turret and a white outline cross on the hull front (217/482/23).

Above left A well-laden StuG III bearing the name 'Leopard'. Its crew are well dressed in the reversible white/mouse grey protective clothing (273/450/23).

Left Crudely whitewashed Tiger I (218/546/4A).

Above 7·5 cm Pak 40 auf GW Lorraine Schlepper (f), ie, a Pak 40 anti-tank gun mounted on a captured French tractor chassis (274/451/17A).

Right StuG III and an SdKfz 252 towing a trailer. Interestingly, the half-track carries the tactical device for a towed artillery unit but the trailer bears that of an SP formation (271/315/17).

Left PzKpfw IVEs of the 7th Panzer Division in convoy (267/141/26).

Below left PzKpfw IVF2 and StuG III (235/962/7A).

Right PzKpfw IVF2 in rather crude snow camouflage (236/1003/28).

Below Miscellany of headquarters tanks of an unidentified unit, including a PzKpfw II, III and two '38(t)s (267/139/23A).

Inset above Abandoned Russian T-26 makes a good signpost !
Prominent on its turret rear is the insignia of the 18th Panzer
Division (212/232/36).

Inset above Panzer-Grenadiers, the foremost figure carrying an MG 34 and well wrapped in his poncho or camouflage shelter quarter, hitch a ride aboard a PzKpfw IV (213/278/12).

Background photograph Nebelwerfers firing at night (216/449/16A).

Left SdKfz 222 leads a convoy over a bridge. Note wooden fascines strapped to the front to assist in mud or snow. This vehicle carries the barred arrow of 23rd Panzer Division on its mudguard (217/455/4A).

Below left That the 8·8 cm Flak was well able to operate while still 'limbered' is clearly shown in this example, which has four aircraft to its credit (216/427/13A).

Above right 7·5 cm Pak 40 auf Fgst PzKpfw II (Sf) or, in other words, a Marder II, said to have been photographed in the Crimea during the winter of 1942 (235/975/4).

Right StuG IIIs of an unidentified unit (221/671A/38).

Below Early Marder III with centrally mounted 76·2 mm (r) gun (217/485/28).

Left PzKpfw IIIs preceding a PzKpfw IV, all thoroughly camouflaged against the snow (215/358/32).

Below left This shot of a PzKpfw III is especially useful to modellers as it shows the 'sit' of the suspension on uneven ground (214/349/20A).

Right PzKpfw III with short-barrelled 5 cm gun. The commander wears one of the popular fur caps (215/370/13).

Below Clear shot of a PzKpfw IVF2 of the 9th Panzer Division (216/404/30).

Above The crew of an SdKfz 250 take cover behind the protective bulk of a Russian T-70 light tank (218/503/19).

Below A motor cycle despatch rider approaches the crew of a sIG 33 auf PzKpfw IB (211/164/17A).

German tanks in use 1941–43

PzKpfw I Ausf B 74 of these early PzKpfw I light tanks were still in use in 1941 but they were rapidly phased out. Weighing 5·8 tons, they had a crew of two, were armed with twin 7·92 MG 13 machine-guns, had armour plate from 6 to 13 mm and a top speed of 40 km/h.

PzKpfw I Ausf C Only two of these vehicles saw service in Russia, being allocated to 1st Panzer Division for evaluation. They were a totally different design with interleaved and overlapping road wheels and increased armour protection up to 30 mm thick. Crewed by two and weighing 8 tons, they were armed with an EW 141 and an MG 34 machine-gun and could achieve a respectable 79 km/h.

PzKpfw II Ausf a and b These early PzKpfw II light tank variants were employed in limited numbers with the reconnaissance battalions in the Panzer divisions in Russia. Very similar in appearance, they were crewed by three men, armed with a single 20 mm KwK 30 and an MG 34, had armour plate between five and 15 mm thick, weighed 7·6 and 7·9 tons respectively and could travel at 40 km/h.

PzKpfw II Aus c, A, B and C The Ausf c was the final development model in the PzKpfw II series and featured a new suspension system with larger road wheels than in the Ausf a and b versions. This system was used on the main Ausf A, B and C production variants. There were only minor differences between all four types. Weighing 8·9 tons and with armour plate up to 16 mm thick, their other characteristics were identical with those quoted above for the Ausf a and b.

PzKpfw II Ausf D and E A different design again, with Christie-type suspension which gave increased speed (55 km/h). They were all converted to flamethrowing vehicles, a few of which saw service in Russia as evidenced by the rare picture on page 42.

PzKpfw II Ausf F Differed from the A–C only in having a one-piece flat front plate 30 mm thick. The weight increased to 9·5 tons, all other factors as above.

PzKpfw II Ausf J Seven of these vehicles saw service with the 12th Panzer Division in Russia. Extra armour protection increased the weight to 18 tons and reduced the speed to 31 km/h, the plating now ranging from 25 to 80 mm making this variant a medium tank in all but name. Crew and weapons as for the earlier versions.

PzKpfw II Ausf L (Luchs) The final refinement of the PzKpfw II series, of which only 100 were built. Based on the Ausf G design which never saw active service, it had a crew of four, armour plate from 10 to 30 mm thickness and a top speed of 60 km/h. Armament was the same 20 mm gun and MG 34 machine-gun as in earlier versions.

PzKpfw 35(t) This Czech design was used in the opening stages of Operation Barbarossa, during which the majority of vehicles were lost. It carried a crew of four, weighed 10·5 tons, had armour protection varying between 8 and 25 mm and could travel at 35 km/h. Armament was the 3·7 cm KwK 34(t) supplemented by two 7·92 mm MG 37(t) machine-guns.

PzKpfw 38(t) Another, and more successful, Czech design, this vehicle was produced in Ausf A to G and S variants, all of which were basically similar with minor variations in vision port and aerial positions. A very well designed light/medium tank, it was crewed by four men, weighed between 9·4 and 10·5 tons, and was armed with the 3·7 cm KwK 34(t) or 38(t). Armour thickness varied between versions from 8 to 50 mm and top speed was 42 km/h. This vehicle later provided the basis for the equally successful Hetzer Jagdpanzer.

PzKpfw III Ausf F The early PzKpfw III Ausf A–E designs did not apparently see service in Russia. The Ausf F was a 19·8-ton vehicle armed with a 3·7 cm gun and two or three MG 34 machine-guns. Crewed by five men, it had armour plate between 12 and 30 mm thick and was capable of a top speed of 40 km/h.

PzKpfw III Ausf G Weighing 20·3 tons and armed with the 5 cm KwK L/42 gun, this vehicle was otherwise similar to the Ausf F.

PzKpfw III Ausf H Around 300 of these vehicles were involved in the invasion of Russia. Basically similar to the Ausf G, they had additional appliqué armour up to a total of 60 mm, revised transmission and a rear turret basket.

PzKpfw III Ausf J First sent to Russia in September 1941, the Ausf J weighed 21·5 tons and had improved armour plate, a ball-mounted bow machine-gun and revised hatches and visors, but was otherwise similar to the Ausf H. Later variants were armed with a 5 cm KwK 39 L/60 gun instead of the L/42 version.

PzKpfw III Ausf L This frontally up-armoured PzKpfw III had integral armour up to 57 mm thick plus 20 mm appliqué on the superstructure front and (sometimes) mantlet. It weighed 22·7 tons and externally differed from earlier variants mainly in the deletion of the lower hull escape hatches. Some 600 of these tanks were in service in Russia at the beginning of the summer 1942 offensive.

PzKpfw III Ausf M This design was supplied to the Panzer divisions in Russia at the end of the period covered by this book and fought at Kursk. The basic differences between it and the Ausf L were the fording equipment, placement of smoke dischargers on the turret sides and, in some cases, provision of hull side and turret Schürzen.

PzKpfw III Ausf N As with the Ausf M, this PzKpfw III variant appeared on the Russian front just in time for the battle of Kursk, where 155 vehicles fought. It was virtually the same as the Ausf M but carried a 7·5 cm KwK L/24 gun instead of the 5 cm L/60 and weighed 23 tons.

PzKpfw III (Flamm) This tank was designed specifically for operations such as Stalingrad but never reached von Paulus' troops. It was virtually identical to the Ausf M apart from the replacement of the 5 cm gun by a 14 mm flamethrower.

PzKpfw IV Ausf B Only 44 of these were produced and, although they saw limited service in Russia, they had been phased out by late 1943. Carrying a crew of five, they were armed with a 7·5 cm KwK 37 L/24 and an MG 34 and could travel at 40 km/h. Weighing 18·8 tons, they had armour plate from 5 to 30 mm thick.

PzKpfw IV Ausf C Minor changes brought the weight of this variant to 19 tons, otherwise identical to the Ausf B.

PzKpfw IV Ausf D Increased armour plate (up to 35 mm) brought the weight of this version up to 20 tons.

PzKpfw IV Ausf E A new cupola design and yet more armour protection brought the weight of this tank to 21 tons.

PzKpfw IV Ausf F1 Although similar at first sight to previous PzKpfw IV variants, this vehicle featured much increased armour protection (up to 50 mm), wider tracks and revised vision ports, etc. It weighed 22·3 tons.

PzKpfw IV Ausf F2 The first PzKpfw IV variant to be armed with a long-barrelled 7·5 cm (L/43) weighed 23 tons but was otherwise virtually indistinguishable from the F1.

PzKpfw IV Ausf G Introduced on the Russian front during the summer of 1942, the G was basically a modified F2 with revised muzzle brake, no turret side vision ports, a new cupola and other minor modifications. Later Ausf Gs were essentially indistinguishable from the Ausf H.

PzKpfw IV Ausf H Weighing in at 25 tons, this version had a 7·5 cm LA/48 gun and featured side and turret Schürzen. It started entering service in April 1943.

PzKpfw V Ausf D This early Panther first saw action during the battle of Kursk (see volume 12 in this series), although it was introduced earlier.

PzKpfw VI Ausf E The Tiger I first saw action on the Leningrad front in August 1942. This heavy tank weighed 57 tons and was crewed by five men. It was armed with the 8·8 cm KwK 36 L/56 gun and featured armour plate between 25 and 100 mm thick. Although unmanoeuvrable and mechanically unreliable, it was capable of some 38 km/h.

Full details of the above and all other German AFVs are available in the superb book by Peter Chamberlain and Hilary Doyle entitled *Encyclopaedia of German Tanks of World War 2*, which is published by Arms and Armour Press. It should be noted that the above list only includes what modern jargon describes as 'main battle tanks' – there were many variants on the same basic chassis, including command and recovery vehicles and self-propelled guns, etc. The list also excludes second line ex-French, etc, tanks.

Other titles in the same series

No 1 Panzers in the Desert
by Bruce Quarrie

No 2 German Bombers over England
by Bryan Philpott

No 3 Waffen-SS in Russia
by Bruce Quarrie

No 4 Fighters Defending the Reich
by Bryan Philpott

No 5 Panzers in North-West Europe
by Bruce Quarrie

No 6 German Fighters over the Med
by Bryan Philpott

No 7 German Paratroops in the Med
by Bruce Quarrie

No 8 German Bombers over Russia
bt Bryan Philpott

No 10 German Fighters over England
by Bryan Philpott

In preparation

No 11 U-Boats in the Atlantic
by Paul Beaver

No 12 Panzers in Russia 1943-45
by Bruce Quarrie

No 13 German Bombers over the Med
by Bryan Philpott

No 14 German Capital Ships
by Paul Beaver

No 15 German Mountain Troops
by Bruce Quarrie

No 16 German Fighters over Russia
by Bryan Philpott

No 17 E-Boats and Coastal Craft
by Paul Beaver

No 18 German Maritime Aircraft
by Bryan Philpott

No 19 Panzers in the Balkans and Italy
by Bruce Quarrie

No 20 German Destroyers and Escorts
by Paul Beaver